Every Student Has a Story

Personal Narratives from First-Generation College Students

Volume II

TRIO Student Support Services

Coordinated & Edited by
Shubitha Kever and Karen Lenfestey

Cover Photo by
Shubitha Kever

ISBN-10: 1548796476
ISBN-13: 978-1548796471

Selena Andrade   Bailey Berndt   Krystal Bendele
Breanna Putt   Cordell England   D'Jara Culpepper
Gabriela Romo   Guerda Julien   Jessica Camarena
Jo'Male Collier   Kayla Frick   Kristin Costello
Lorenzo Catalan   Megan Pearsall   Miranda Hall
Riley Erck   Tayah Luckadoo   Tiffany Lackey
Yin Thet   Anita Vannatta   Karen Lenfestey
Shubitha Kever

DEDICATION

When you're the first person in your family to do something, many obstacles can stand in your way. This book is dedicated to all the first-generation college students who struggle to fit-in, who sometimes wonder if they should quit, but who persevere and work diligently to succeed and overcome.

CONTENTS

INTRODUCTION

This book is a compilation of essays by TRIO Student Support Services Students at Indiana University Purdue University Fort Wayne (IPFW). Inspired by Aquinas College's student publishing project, IPFW TRIO Student Support Services completed its first book of essays in 2016. This book is the second volume and a follow up to the first book. Students who participated were asked to share their stories, listen to other students' stories, and get help crafting their stories into compelling essays—highlighting their life experiences. Students were simply asked:

What has it been like for you being the first person in your family to go to college?

What struggles have you faced and what have you learned from those struggles?

Over the last two years, the stories and subsequent essays these questions generated far exceeded the project's initial expectations. Essays from year two students are now combined in this powerful second volume in the hope that they will resonate with other first-generation students who often feel as though they don't fit in and who struggle but keep pressing forward.

This process has helped students develop meaningful friendships with their peers and gain a greater sense of self-confidence in their writing abilities. But even more importantly, this process has cultivated a greater sense of pride for students related to their personal experiences and their many successes and triumphs.

DECISIONS, DECISIONS
BY SELENA ANDRADE

Tacos, "Norteña" music, Quinceañeras, Our Lady of Guadalupe…McDonalds, pop music, county fairs, Big Foot… These things, and others, are the things that I grew up eating, listening to, attending, and believing in as a Mexican-American. As a child, I was lucky enough to learn both the English language and the Spanish language. Coming from a Latino background comes with a lot of advantages. For example, the food is great! And, on a serious note, there will always be jobs for people who speak both English and Spanish. Unfortunately, with those advantages also comes personal disadvantages.

As a child, both of my parents worked and did not have the time to teach me basic concepts like the alphabet, counting numbers, and the colors. Fortunately, I had my brother, Sesame Street, and all of the other PBS children's shows. When I was about 10, my brother moved out and I had to deal with homework on my own. I always pushed myself to get good grades in elementary and middle school because I wanted to make my parents and my brother proud. I wanted to secure success in high school so I could get into a good college.

When I finally got into high school, my parents stressed to "always put in the effort." They often talk about how they never had the privilege to continue schooling after the third and fifth grades. That makes me sad that they could not finish school. They remind me that they do what they do to secure a better life for me. They do not want me working in a factory in bad conditions like they do. I see their determination and their hard work, and I feel bad. I feel like they never got to live their youth the proper way. They come from big families; so when they were younger, their parents needed their help doing chores on the farm. When they became of age, they got married and wanted a better life for their future kids, so they came here to the U.S. in search of the American Dream. They told me their hair-raising story crossing the border and their struggles getting their proper documentation to be able to stay here. At first, they could not find good paying jobs. They willingly accepted labor-intensive jobs so they could reach that American Dream. I feel like it is my job to pay them back for all of their hard work. That is why I push myself. That is why their words are engraved in my head to always put in the effort.

All throughout high school, I was fascinated with cultures and their histories. At that time, I did not know what I wanted to study in college. My parents pushed me to do something in the medical field, but those dreams were soon crushed after I came home one day after I volunteered at the St. Joseph Regional Medical Center's emergency department. I discovered that I could not handle other people's blood and that there was no way I could be a nurse. I felt like a failure. I had ruined the perfect image that my parents had proudly described to my extended family. I could hear it now, the "Oh mija, you should still stick to the medical field." Luckily, that did not happen. My parents were still determined to put me through college no matter what I would study. I thank my brother for that. I believe he had a major role in convincing my parents to have faith in me.

As I entered college, I had graphic design and criminal justice in the back of my head as potential fields of study. My freshman year of college, I had the privilege to take a variety of classes to see what interested me. In high school, I had taken dual credit classes that counted as both high school and college credits. So, I basically was a semester ahead. I learned in that first semester that although I did enjoy the class, I did not want anything to do with criminal justice. There were too many legal factors and I could not keep one law straight from the other. As for graphic design, I realized I had trouble being creative. Toward the end of my first semester, my academic advisor wanted me to declare a major. I panicked. I remember crying to my parents and telling them sorry because I was a failure. I had worked so hard in middle and high school for nothing. I had no idea what to do! Neither of my parents went to college, so they did not understand my frustration. They never had to stay up past midnight to work on calculus or to write a 7-8-page paper over the material learned in sociology. All I could think of was how my parents were wasting their money on me and how disappointed they would be to have to tell my extended family that their "bright" daughter dropped out of college.

My mother has the gift of encouragement. That woman can make the toughest thing look easy. She told me to quit crying because she knew that I was smart. She said to keep searching potential career paths. She told me that she did not care how long it took me to figure it out because God has a plan for me. She was sure that I would find something that would spark my interest. Sure enough, just before I had to declare my major, my friend told me about the hospitality program at IPFW. I was intrigued. I loved serving people at my old job at Dairy Queen, back in high school; and, I did not mind the idea of working in a hotel or resort in some place exotic, so I declared that as my major. I took the intro classes and instantly loved it.

My goal is to graduate with a Bachelor of Science degree in Hospitality and Tourism Management and afterwards find a job that will allow me to work internationally—possibly in a resort in Spain or on a cruise line. Recently, I have taken some culinary classes that have really sparked my interest in international cuisines. I can also thank the Mexican culture for sparking this interest as well. I like to note the differences that other Latino dishes have compared to the Mexican dishes. I also do that with other cultures. It amazes me how similar, yet different they all are.

I can say that growing up Mexican-American has definitely shaped my life in a creative way. At one end I am lucky to have my Mexican heritage, and at the other, I am lucky to have grown up in the American culture. It is a struggle sometimes to recognize my personal identity because I have two major cultures clashing against each other. Should I act this way or should I act that way? In the end, no matter the culture struggles I have, I would not change my life. I thank my parents for bringing me to the U.S. and putting me through college. If it were not for them, I would be illiterate and milking a cow 2,000 miles away. Instead, I get to enjoy Quinceañera celebrations and Fourth of July fireworks—tacos and hot dogs. I am lucky to be Mexican-American.

FOUR STARS
BY BAILEY BERNDT

Being a first-generation college student puts a lot of weight on your shoulders. I was concerned about doing well in my classes and was overly eager to fit in. At first, it was difficult for me to adjust to college because A) I don't make friends very easily (I graduated high school with one friend); B) I commuted to campus like many other students at IPFW; and C) I wasn't too gung-ho about being on a campus. My goal in high school was to get in and get out while excelling in my art classes. That mentality had transferred over.

I started my college experience on a rather unsure foot. On my first day, I drove to campus about an hour early before my classes because I didn't want to be late. I over-thought the homework and projects, and I went through five colored pens while putting together my calendar. However, I really enjoyed the homework that I was doing. At one point, I thought, "Heck yeah, I'm mastering this whole college thing." I was only a month in. Overly confident was my mentality.

I got to winter break and the social aspect of my life started to pick up. I became a founding member of Alpha Sigma Alpha, a sorority on-campus. I wore my letters, went to sisterhood events, and participated in different ceremonies and observances for the sorority. I got really involved with my "sisters" and built a new friend group—the complete opposite of how I felt in high school. I wasn't the stereotypical sorority girl, though. Our chapter (Iota Delta) and other chapters of the sorority had no tolerance for hazing or partying. Anything to tarnish the name of the school, the group, or the person was a no go. Those rules were set by our headquarters and I was so grateful for that. I also became the vice president of the Interior Design Club. I was stacking up titles and experiences to put on my résumé.

At some point in the second semester, I decided that I wanted more time for myself. I was overworked and needed to relax. Side note—really bad idea. That late into the semester is not a good time to take a break. Like at all. At this time of the semester, you should be working hard and long hours to get final projects done so you can move on to the next one.

Now you might be wondering how difficult can an interior design major's course load be? Um...hard, really hard. There were lots of projects that involved studying color combinations, modeling, and writing backgrounds of imaginary clients. Yes, all these things and more have to be done before displaying the work. Not to mention, I had many of the same professors for all of my classes. Their projects would meld together and sometimes I wouldn't know if I was studying materials or identifying patterns.

The sorority, homework, and my part-time job took up most of my time. I was in meetings in-between classes for the sorority; then, I would run to class; and after class, I would go to work or stay on campus and pull late hours doing projects. I would stare at my computer screen squinting at models, listening to the ever-annoying clicking of my mouse as the time slipped by.

By then, I had really gotten used to being on campus. Maybe a tad too comfortable. I spent one night in the library. It was almost 10 o'clock and I started to laugh because I had spent almost 4 hours on the same model and was no closer to finishing it than I had been when I first started. There was no one in the library and there was no chance my professor would answer her email this late. (She wouldn't answer them anyway.) It was all me. I sat there and just stared off into space, paced around the book shelves, and avoided the work for at least a half hour. I thought, "Maybe if I go get food I will think better." That was a big NO! I was still stuck. "This is my life now. I am destined to sit in this spot until I get it finished." I immediately packed my things and left. I was not going to live in the library. I refused.

At one point, I calculated how much time I would need to finish all my projects a week in advance so I could relax and not stress myself out. Now I'm not a math major, but even I could figure out that would be a lot of hours of work-plus a lot of coffee-minus sleep-minus a social life to equal exhausted Bailey and tear-stained project boards. (I would have to redo the projects anyway, if that happened.)

So, second semester meant learning a lesson about balance and the importance of managing my social life with time for myself. All of which, I was horrible at. I finally gained control of my schedule, my obligations, and my freedom. It only took me an entire year.

Putting all of that aside, I really couldn't have asked for a better freshman year. I was emotionally and physically exhausted; and, I really didn't care because I had done more than what was expected of me. I got firsthand experience in college life; I joined a Greek sorority and proudly wore my letters; I became an officer in a club; and,

I went to work on my days off from class. I had voluntarily signed up for exhaustion. I, however, did not party and I also didn't gain the mythical freshman fifteen.

Now, I have a feel for the ins and outs of what college life is like and am better prepared for the coming years. I know tricks to scheduling classes and where to nap on campus. I also learned that there are resources on campus that I had never even realized existed. That was the most valuable information I could have gained from my freshman year. If I had to give my college freshman year a Yelp review, it would be 4 stars. I would unquestionably go again.

A ROAD WORTH TRAVELING
BY KRYSTAL BENDELE

My road to academic success was not an easy one. I had a speech impediment and attended speech therapy from the age of three. The speech therapy continued after I began school; and unfortunately, my appointments were during reading lessons. I fell behind very quickly in reading. Then, I received reading services but during another academic course: math. By the time I was in second grade, I was so far behind in all subjects that my mother kept me home for a semester and home-schooled. With her help, I had caught up to my peers; but shortly after returning to the school system, I began falling behind again.

Since I did not want to be pulled out of classes again, I faked being able to read. During quiet reading time, I would scan the book and turn the pages along with my classmates. When a teacher would ask about what I had read, I would paraphrase what I had heard other students say. By the time I was in tenth grade, I read at a third grade level. My mother had high hopes for me to attend college, but I was not even sure if I could graduate high school.

Fortunately in tenth grade, I had a literature teacher who recognized that I was functionally illiterate. He insisted I read anything that appealed to me. I began reading science fiction, slowly at first, then avidly. By the end of tenth grade, I was reading at grade level. But at the end of my senior year, I still had not earned the credits to graduate. Friends, classmates, and even a few relatives asked why did I not just drop out and get my GED. I ignored them. I had just begun to see the future I wanted, and I was not going to be swayed. It took five years, but I graduated high school.

After graduation, I decided to raise the bar. I set the goal of earning an associate degree in criminal justice, and I achieved this goal at the age of 26. Then, I took a year to look for work but realized I wanted more education. My new goal is to finish my bachelor's degree and apply for graduate school. My career goal is to work in the criminal justice system as a profiler or detective.

There have been many times when I was not sure I would succeed; but now, knowing how close I am to my goal, I am inspired to keep going. The struggles I faced at the beginning of my academic career are far behind and new exciting challenges await. If I could give my younger self advice, I would let her know that it is okay to be frustrated by obstacles. Learn to kick them down and make them your bridge. Most importantly, I would tell her: the road to success may be a rocky one, but it is worth the journey.

JUST DO IT
BY BREANNA RENÉ PUTT

As a senior in college, I started to realize all the things I wish I would've done differently. Now, I reflect back on the last four years of college and see what I have gotten out of it and all the things I missed out on. While in college, I was always working 2-3 jobs while still taking 15-18 credit hours. This kept me busy and made it hard to try and get involved in more social activities in college. It also didn't help that I used to be a very shy person. I wouldn't talk to anyone because I'd be afraid they'd judge me or that I just wouldn't fit in. I also overthought everything and wouldn't want to be 'rude' and intrude on someone's 'clique.' My first couple years of college I spent little time on campus. I would go to my classes and that was that. I wouldn't stay for the programs or any events that were going on because I didn't know anybody, and I didn't want to put myself out there. I didn't want to be that awkward person who just showed up at an event all by herself. Before I knew it, I was in my final year of college and felt like I'd missed out on a lot.

When I joined TRIO, it helped me come out of my

shell more and actually talk to others. However, it wasn't until my last two years of college that I really started getting more involved with TRIO and going to more social events. TRIO helped me to grow as a person; and having an advisor who really cared that I succeeded and could talk to, helped give me confidence in the decisions I was making while going through college. I was able to meet positive people who all had their own goals in how they wanted to succeed. I felt more comfortable striking up conversations with others without feeling like a bother. I realized that after all these years I had underestimated how welcoming others could be.

I still worked 2 jobs while getting more involved in school programs and clubs; but, I still wish I would've done more. I did end up joining TRIO Club which helped me volunteer and do more for the community. Thanks to TRIO Club, I was given the chance to travel to Puerto Rico and get the experience of a lifetime. While in Puerto Rico, I was able to see how different things can be in other places—such as—the buildings being built differently and being more colorful and vibrant than here in America. It was neat seeing how people interacted with each other and what was considered cultural norms was also quite interesting. Being able to travel with others who are on the same mission as you to help out and volunteer where they can, was amazing. Being able to experience the cultural diversity firsthand, as well as, experiencing the language barrier is an experience I will cherish for as long as I can remember.

Looking back now, all I can do is reflect on my college years and see what I could have done differently. I am proud of how far I have come since starting college and being able to graduate with two degrees, debt-free. I have become more outgoing by putting myself in awkward and uncomfortable situations which have actually helped me grow as a person. For example, this past semester, I joined a sport league because someone I went to high school with randomly messaged me about needing a girl for their team. Before I overthought it, I replied I would do it. However, when the time came closer to actually go to the game and be on a team with six other people I did not know, I got nervous. I wanted to back out. But, I didn't. I went and made great new friends; and, we hang out still to this day. I wouldn't change it for the world.

My advice? Get out there, put yourself in uncomfortable situations. Make conversation, talk to people. The worst thing someone can do is reject you or ignore you, but you know what? There are billions of other people who will accept you for who you are and that is what matters. If you want to do something but you're afraid it will be awkward, just do it. Don't live life wishing you would have done something because building relationships and having friends helps make college better. It is a stress reliever. Do what you want and never talk yourself out of something that could lead to an opportunity to grow.

Breanna Putt earned a bachelor's degree in public policy with a major in health administration, a major in criminal justice, and a minor in public affairs in December 2016. She earned a second bachelor's degree in general studies and minor in economics in May 2017.

MAY THEY REST IN PEACE
BY CORDELL ENGLAND

Being a first-generation college student has not been easy. My parents divorced when I was young and drugs have been around in my family ever since I was born. Both my mom and dad wanted me to go to college and be successful as most parents want for their kids. I graduated high school and was not sure what to expect when I came to college. My first semester was tough because I took a business calculus class and I have never experienced a harder class. Not only that, but in October my sister passed away of a heroin overdose. She was one of my biggest supporters going through high school; and, she was so happy and couldn't wait for me to start my new life at college. But, she will not get to see it now; so, I keep her in my prayers every day and do things in life trying to be successful—knowing that I get to see her again one day.

After she died, it was super hard for me to keep going to class and to get good grades. She used to call me from time-to-time asking, all jokingly, if I was partying a lot or skipping classes. Little did I know, I wouldn't get those calls any more. I ended up dropping my math class and was going to try again in the spring semester.

At 2:30 in the morning on Monday, January 9, 2017, I woke up to a call from my aunt, saying that my mom had just passed away. She had been dealing with a severe case of cirrhosis—due to past years of alcoholism—and, some early signs of dementia. It had been extremely hard knowing that she didn't have much time; but, I did not want to accept the fact that her time was coming to pass. That Monday morning when I got the call was the first day of spring classes. For me, it was not easy to go to classes. I was tempted not to go, but I knew I was going to have to go at some point and I wanted my professors to have a good impression of me. Math class was already hard enough and I didn't want to get behind. On the other hand when I went to class, my mind was somewhere else. It was terrible for me because I had to act like everything was okay. It was also hard because I had to focus on all six of my classes and keep up with my job. It was hard to go to class; it was hard to get dressed; honestly, it was hard for me to even want to be in college or be with anyone at the time. I remember a couple days after my mom had passed, I just sat in my car in silence for hours in the parking lot. I couldn't tell if I was mad, sad, or just down right pissed. I didn't know what to feel; I just felt lost.

Even though those major things happened in my life, I still managed to keep my grades up (except for math). I am keeping a positive outlook for my future and trying to do the best I can in school. With the help of my girlfriend, friends, family, and especially my TRIO advisor, I have managed to stay on track and am better prepared for my sophomore year here at IPFW. To anyone and everyone who is reading this or hearing this: keep your head up because if you ever need an ear, I got you; I promise.

DEAR FRESHMAN SELF
BY D'JARA CULPEPPER

Much has happened in two semesters. When I last saw
you, you were practically sure you would switch your
major from Mechanical Engineering to Mechanical
Engineering Technology (M.E.T.) in the fall of 2016. I can
confidently tell you that this is **not** what happened at all!
You might be confused by all this, at the very least; and I
am too, in my own way. I am writing to you because it is
time we reflect on our grand adventure – the hard times,
the places where we could have done better, the places
where we improved, and all of the in-between places along
the way.

Coming into college, you just *knew* you wanted to be an
engineer – well, you knew that you had other interests, but
engineering was your goal. It felt like a given; you had
studied engineering throughout high school and you loved
knowing how to put things together and make them work.
One math requirement was giving you the blues back then
(calculus), so you retook it in college…twice. You worked
hard and went to tutoring sessions when you were getting
lost in the math; you just didn't always "get" it. And

obviously, your other courses couldn't slow down just so you could focus on that one class, either. If we're honest, you neglected some important things during this frustrating wrinkle in time: some classes and assignments, personal responsibilities, your hygiene! Your fall and spring semesters were nearly identical: some of your grades were great while others were Cs or Ds. Despite trying to balance out your workload, you weren't happy and you felt stupid to the point of not feeling worthy to go to college. You didn't see this coming, right? You just knew M.E.T. would be easier for you after that last meeting with your advisor (less calculus and more visual); and yet, you had no actual idea where things were heading for you.

Fortunately amongst all of the negatives, I have some good news for us. Well, I guess I should say, I have some strange good news. For instance, we started working on our M.E.T. credits in the fall of our sophomore year but ended up failing our physics course... That's not good news, or is it? Sure, things could have been done better, especially on the assignments given, but it wasn't because we didn't try at all. We went to our professor for help when we really didn't understand things—even when that help hadn't gotten us too far in the past. The point is, we didn't quit. We kept trying 'til the end. Here's another bit of news – we're an English major now! "WHAT?! How did that even happen? *Is* this a good thing?" is what you're probably thinking. I can only answer that in multiple parts.

To start, let's not sound so nonchalant – we've been writing poetry for **fun** since elementary school. I don't believe in fate, but the transition felt somewhat natural when we finally switched majors, as if this was bound to happen eventually. I won't lie to you; there have been a few challenges. I only said "somewhat" before for a reason. The amount of guilt that we felt for switching majors hasn't completely disappeared; it shows up randomly to this day. Our reading comprehension has not proven to be a problem for once, but our speed has – we still read rather slowly and it can be hard to keep up. Thankfully, when it comes to novels especially, there have been free audiobooks online for most of the texts we've read thus far; those have helped us keep up. Lastly, we could potentially get to write and talk about all of the great works we loved early on and then some. I say this because we've covered some work by two of our favorite writers so far. It has proven difficult at times, but it *is* work at the end of the day, even if we love the subject matter to death. We just need to learn to let go and move on to the next text and assignment, even when you aren't ready to.

So, freshman self, I just want you to know that you will get through that first year, maybe a bit battered, but persevere, you will. I know I have said some vague things and might not have all of the answers you've been seeking; but I'm telling you, kid, we're close. I have made plenty of mistakes in this second year, but I've learned so much already and I'm feeling a bit more comfortable in my skin. I honestly believe, we can do this college thing after all.

ECHALE PURAS GANAS (GIVE IT YOUR BEST)
BY GABRIELA ROMO

The door to the trailer creaks open and my six-year-old heart races, hoping that today my father will not take his frustration out on my three brothers and me. As he sits down, I hand him the remote for the television and remove his shoes to massage his feet. There is no eruption of violence. Soon, my mother comes home and I repeat the same service while my brothers play. She never hits me, but she is exhausted every day.

Bills, chores, economic struggle, and fear were the center of my childhood. Even though it was difficult sometimes, I am proud I could help my parents. I was aware of the poor working conditions at their factory jobs and knew they came home, day after day, tired and frustrated. Even today, when they are sick, they still must work. I once pleaded, "Mom, don't go to work tomorrow. You need to rest to get better." With dark circles under her eyes, she cried, "You and your brothers are my motivation. I have to work so you have food in your stomachs, clothes on your backs, and a roof over your heads." Then she cupped my chin and insisted, "This is why you need to focus on school. I don't want you to depend on a man and I don't want to see you end up like us—working like mules."

Fortunately, soccer was an escape from all the stressors in my life, and my dream then was to be a professional soccer player. My career aspirations changed when my mother had a surgery that could have been prevented by a healthier diet. As the primary caretaker of my mother, I realized health has a domino effect. Being sick prevented her from going to work, which then impeded her from providing for herself and for her family. Several studies indicate that preventative medicine can improve and sustain quality health for everyone. I have interacted with less educated people locally and abroad who, unfortunately, think their poor and unsanitary living conditions are normal. I now want to educate individuals that social determinants like environmental hazards can affect their health and I want to be able to offer preventative health to them.

At the time of my mother's surgery, I was in the International Baccalaureate program at Goshen High School taking biology with an amazing teacher who gave me the opportunity to participate in a marine biology trip to Florida. I realized the interconnectedness of the world: everything I saw had a biological role on our health whether directly or indirectly. I learned it is not only what we see but also what we do not see that can affect our health. Once I learned about microorganisms, I was hungry to understand their medical role in the human microbiome.

My new passion for medicine was solidified when my cousin died from a preventable disease. The doctors in Mexico would not see her without payment. Since my cousin's family lived in poverty, I took the economic responsibility and sent all my money from my summer factory job. By the time the money arrived, the illness had progressed too far. An untreated cough caused by a bacterium led to the death of a beloved single mother of five children.

Despite this passion for human medicine, I was hesitant to pursue a career in healthcare due to negative experiences with healthcare. Those physicians did not provide whole-person care and did not partner with my family to find solutions that would work with our lifestyle and financial limitations. It is because of these frustrating experiences, I now aspire to build stronger relationships with my future patients in order to provide empathic, individualized care. While learning about health disparities, my findings showed that the healthcare system actively works against poor minorities and those in rural areas; this sparked my medical passion even more.

I gained hope of becoming a physician after interacting with a physician from a local clinic who worked for underserved communities. Translating for him allowed me to connect the patient and the healthcare team. As a translator, I had first-hand experience in developing empathy and cultural competence in a clinical setting. The physician would tell me step-by-step what he wanted to learn from the interaction with the patient while he practiced cultural humility. He would plan a regimen that would treat and prevent further illnesses while taking into account social determinant factors. I admire this physician and the work he does and have now set it as a goal to strive to help transform the healthcare system into a system of equity.

I am very blessed to say I am a student-athlete graduate from IPFW. I majored in biology with concentrations in microbiology and immunology and minored in psychology. After commencement, I will be pursuing my dual degree of MD/MPH the fall of 2017 at the Indiana University School of Medicine. I aspire to become a family physician for underserved communities, especially for the Hispanic population. With my master's degree in public health, I plan to combine this knowledge with my medical knowledge to serve patients individually and at a community level.

I used to imagine myself scoring a goal in front of thousands of fans in a beautiful stadium. Now, I imagine myself saving a valuable life. After I massage my mother's feet today, she cups my chin and says, "I'm proud that you have found your passion. Now don't let anyone take it away. Echale puras ganas."

MON LONG VOYAGE
(MY LONG JOURNEY)
BY GUERDA JULIEN

I became a nun and entered a convent in 1975 in Haiti where I worked as a school principal. In 2000, I had eye surgery which left me blind. When I came to visit my family in the United States, my nephew took me to an eye doctor who explained what was wrong. It took five surgeries, and now I can see well enough to read large print. Due to all of the necessary follow-up doctor visits, I needed to stay in the United States. I lived in a convent in Ohio for nine years; but when I had more issues with my eyes, I moved to Indiana where my family could take me to the doctor. When I left Ohio, it was difficult for me to pay my medical bills and all of my other living expenses. Last semester, I had a short hospital stay, which added to my bills. I have been going to college part-time since 2009 and I will graduate this year. Even though I work 55 hours a week, I am determined to earn my bachelor's degree. I already have an associate's degree, but I believe what I'm learning in psychology and human services will improve my ability to serve patients at my current jobs.

I am a Mental Health Technician at Parkview Behavioral Health and a Direct Support Professional at Easter Seals Arc. Even though I make more money at Parkview, I spend 31 hours a week at Easter Seals because I believe in their mission, allowing the disabled to live with dignity. Helping people feeds my soul. That's why in addition to working full-time and taking 9 credits at IPFW, I volunteer in the community. Last semester, I volunteered in the cafeteria at St. Jude's School to help clean tables and supervise children in grades K-8. There, I discovered two autistic kids who needed my guidance in choosing what to eat first and staying focused. Otherwise, they would be distracted by all of the activity in the cafeteria and forget to eat before they returned to class. In January, I volunteered for Allen County's Rescue Mission Homeless Count. Twice a month, I drive disabled people to and from their Kiwanis Club action committee meetings because if I didn't, they wouldn't be able to attend. In the past, I have also sang in my church choir and helped set up and cook food when people held funerals there.

If it weren't for TRIO Student Support Services first at Ivy Tech and now at IPFW, I don't believe I would have been able to make it in college. I appreciate the way the TRIO staff and other TRIO students make me feel welcome. My success in class depends on the good help TRIO academic coordinators have provided for me. Since English is my second language, sometimes I don't understand my homework assignments—like last year when I needed to make an infographic and I didn't know what that was. When something like that happens, I go to my TRIO advisor and they help explain what the professor wants. In addition to the language issue, I need help using technology and TRIO is there for me. Last summer, I took an online class which required me to use Facebook—which I had never joined. I came into the TRIO office and my advisor walked me through the process. My advisor has also looked at my bills and assisted me in making a budget. One of my favorite parts of TRIO, though, is the cultural trips. These trips are a boost because I don't have the money for vacations and I rarely get time for me. If it weren't for TRIO, I don't know if I could make it.

From blindness to learning a new language, I've faced many obstacles. I appreciate all of the support and encouragement TRIO and the IPFW disabilities center has given me. This year, I will officially finish my education and look forward to utilizing what I've learned to help others. Although it has been a long journey to earn my bachelor's degree, it has enriched my life immensely.

LEARNING A NEW LANGUAGE
BY JESSICA CAMARENA

Communication is a key element in building relationships with people. That, however, can be difficult if you speak a different language. I grew up in a Latino household, where Spanish was the only language spoken by my parents. I began elementary school without knowing any English and this made it hard to make friends. Soon enough, I began to feel very isolated and different. I'm sure many other first-generation Latino students can tell you about their experience of being taken out of the classroom every day to learn English. Even though ESL (English as a Second Language) had good intentions, it soon made me realize how different I was from my peers.

Throughout elementary school, I felt very different which I think made my peers weary of me. I began to self-teach at home by watching cartoons in English to battle the language barrier. Learning English not only allowed me to understand my peers but also helped me gain my confidence back. I was finally able to communicate with my peers and make friends. My closest friends accepted me even though I was different; and for that reason, I will always embrace the uniqueness in others and in myself.

Since I was young, I pushed myself to not let my limited English skills stop me from learning. Soon enough, I was able to accelerate in the classroom and my satisfactory grades turned to excellent. The newfound confidence that learning gave me made me value my education. My parents also contributed to the value of education. Actually, they are the biggest reason I am where I am today. They immigrated to the United States in their teens and neither of them went to college. They have pushed me to excel in school and taught me to always give back. Growing up in the middle class for me, meant having what I needed even though I couldn't always have what I wanted. My parents never let me forget where I came from and how they struggled to get where they are today. Their hard work motivated me to never take things for granted and to always take advantage of opportunities.

I didn't exactly have an easy life but it definitely doesn't compare to what my parents went through and what others still go through. This summer, I had the opportunity of a lifetime to travel to Ecuador on a medical mission's trip where I saw firsthand how difficult life can be. We stayed at a local clinic in a poor fishers' town in San Lorenzo, where crime and poverty is high. The way people live was quite eye opening. Their local stores were protected with bars where you couldn't browse or look around. Kids walked around with no shoes and there were homeless dogs everywhere.

While I was there, I learned a lot about their health care system and the history of the clinic. Most of its growth can be attributed to the general surgeon at the clinic. Her story really inspired and motivated me even more to continue on the healthcare route. She explained to us how she visited Ecuador once and decided she wanted to help the people and she obtained her Ecuadorian medical license to work at the clinic.

When speaking with the locals, I realized how happy they were and how grateful they were to have us there to help the doctor. One of the greatest things I experienced was being able to observe surgeries that people had been waiting a while to get done—whereas in the U.S., they would get done as soon as possible. We did many hernias, gallbladder removals, hysterectomies, and thyroidectomies. It was amazing to see how intricately the doctor worked in each operation and how she cared so much about how the patient was feeling.

Even though it wasn't required, knowing Spanish helped me tremendously in order to communicate with the locals and patients. I was able to use my Spanish speaking skills to also help translate which made me grateful for knowing Spanish. I'm also thankful for having an early language barrier that I learned to overcome because it has shown me that any obstacle in life can be overcome through hard work and dedication. What had once held me back and made me feel different is now an asset.

MY COLLEGE BULLY
BY JO'MALE COLLIER

Can you describe a bully? Picture it in your mind. You might think of a school peer. Someone who stole your lunch money and called you names. My bully wasn't my peer, but he was taking my money, and I was insulted whenever I saw him. My bully was my college professor. He had tenure so he wouldn't be leaving any time soon. His entire class could fail and he would still be here while his students would be left mentally disoriented. This was my second semester of college. I had always viewed myself as intelligent. I still do. In his class the other students feared answering his questions. He told me that I was better off dropping the course. I was faced with the decision of whether to stay and fight or drop. I chose to stay and fight, a small part of me liked to argue and wanted to prove him wrong. Unfortunately, that didn't happen the first semester. I got an F in his course; and according to my advisor, I would have to take his class again during the summer. This had to happen for me to stay on track. I hated this and didn't want to be in his class again.

Fear struck as I entered his class again that summer. I

felt angry and fearful. I felt sorry for the other, naive students walking into the classroom. Many students were in shock after the first day when he had unleashed his verbal assaults. Long story short, this classroom started with around 30 students and ended with only seven. I remember going to his office and asking him what to do when he insulted us. He said, insult him back. He wanted to play a game—literally, this is how he referred to it. In class when I refused to respond, he had said "Oh Joe, you don't want to play?" I don't like games. It has been said to keep your friends close and your enemies closer; so, I decided to go to his office. In the corner, I noticed a chess board and asked if he played. We started a new routine: before each class we played chess. During each class whenever he insulted a student, I insulted him back. I told him, "It takes a shmuck to know a shmuck." Before the first exam, I had made a few mistakes on homework and he looked at me as though nothing had changed. I got the test back and I passed it with a B. He gave me a pat on the back and said, "Good job, Joe." He had completely flipped the script.

From this point on, my confidence was boosted. I used to think he had a bias, and—well, he did. If you got good grades, you were treated well; otherwise, you were bombarded with insults. I now knew both sides of this awful story. The students who were insulted banded together and decided to go the Dean. They asked if I was interested, but I declined. I knew this would go nowhere. Afterwards, the professor then hit them even harder by placing limits on the tutors. They were allowed to do a similar problem but not the homework and there were only so many problems they were allowed to do. I wanted to help because if it were me, I am positive that I would want to be helped. To fail and know you're failing is like drowning without a life boat in sight. You fight and fight but you can't save yourself. As stated before, I got a B on the first exam. After this, I got an A on the other two and an A on the final. Each time I got an A, he would congratulate me.

In the end, I passed the class. I had faced my bully and I won. For others, however, they would have to retake the class for a second or third time. Despite my doubts and despite his insults, I had succeeded. Even when all seemed hopeless, I continued to push and fight. I did this for my dream and to make it a reality. Nothing comes easy in this life; and if it is a dream you have, be willing to fight for it. It will make the victory all the more worthwhile.

NEVER ALONE
BY KAYLA FRICK

Family…family is a huge part of my life. I wouldn't be who I am today if it wasn't for them. My family is what really motivated me to go to college. My dad, my mom, they never went to college. Neither did my brother and he often tells me, "Kayla don't ever give up on college. I did and I've regretted it ever since." I know what all he has gone through from having two kids within a year to working all day to help support his family. I know my parents and brother are proud of me for going to college. I know that when I graduate, they will be there smiling and cheering for me.

The transition into college has been hard for us, especially since I went to college out of state. I went from a small town in Ohio to a big city—Fort Wayne, Indiana. It was hard to leave the support group I'd had my whole life. Suddenly, I was in college and didn't have as much support. I know my family is there for me, but here at college, you have to add to your support group as well. However, it might take you a while to find it or figure out who it is.

In college, who do I consider my support group? I would say my friends are like my family here at college. I know that whatever happens over these next three years that they will be there for me and I for them. Some other people, I believe are in my college family is my professors. I feel this because they want me to succeed and everything they do is getting me one step closer to accomplishing my dreams.

Moving here was hard and a scary choice because I didn't know anyone. But since the school year has progressed, I have been able to go through this year easily and successfully. So yes, I have had some good times and hard times. I don't know what the future holds, but what I do know is that as long as I have my support group behind me, these next three years of college, I will never be alone!!!

A DAY WITHOUT WORK
BY KRISTIN COSTELLO

Growing up, work was a very important part of my life. I was raised in a culture that put work, grades, my success, character and integrity as a priority. I was also taught to work and not to depend on anyone else. By the time my mom was 14, she had a job—and my dad 15. My parents were raised to work for what they wanted and earned everything they needed to get. This was and has been a very important aspect of my entire upbringing.

I began working before the age of 14 years old. I earned my way by cleaning houses, babysitting, and picking up other various jobs from people who needed things. By my 16th birthday, I was working in restaurants and fast food establishments. All throughout high school, I learned to pay my own way. Before I moved away to college, I was already planning and applying to places where I could work while receiving my education.

My freshman year of college, I began with one job, then two—and by junior/senior year, I had as many as three or four jobs at a time. It wasn't just because my parents continued to plant the seed in my head to be a hard worker and work for everything I had, but also because I had no one to depend on but me. College is not cheap. I knew that I could not survive off of grants and scholarships alone. Yes, the cost of living in the city of Fort Wayne was much cheaper than where I was from, but I couldn't pay for all of my expenses with one part-time job by myself.

I thought working nearly full-time throughout high school was tough. I managed my grades and my academics, but when I got to college, I felt like I was burning myself out. While at IPFW, I was always a full-time student. By sophomore year, I was working full-time too. I kept up with my grades and I survived the stress of multiple jobs while still maintaining a very good GPA. Surprisingly, a couple of semesters I even managed to earn a 4.0.

As crazy as it sounds, working so much actually helped me to become better with time management. It helped me to become better organized than I already was by encouraging me to become more active on campus with different clubs, groups, and organizations. I'm not saying that everyone has to work throughout college; but what I learned is that there are others like me, where working is a requirement in order to survive. I did it. I not only managed to work full-time throughout my college career; but, I managed to build my work ethic, have a better life, become a better person and finally earn my degree. It's hard, believe me, I'm not here to tell you that it's easy. I'm just here to encourage you that anything's possible with hard work and determination.

Don't ever get discouraged if you don't have the luxury of going through your four years of college without working a day. It can be stressful, exhausting, draining; but if you have to pull those 18 hours days like I had to, I promise you your four years are going to fly by. The day you have that diploma in your hand, you'll tell yourself it was completely worth every meltdown, every obstacle, every victory, and every learning experience you had along the way. I am here to witness and show you that I am living proof that all things you desire, you can receive. Trust me, if I can do it, I promise, you can do it too.

Kristin Costello graduated in May 2017 with a bachelor's degree in hospitality management and is glad to now only work one full-time job.

TIRED, BROKE, AND HUNGRY
BY LORENZO CATALAN

My first college award letter, which included the scholarships I had worked so hard for back in high school, had more money on that piece of paper than my family made in an entire year. No, I didn't have a full ride, nor did I have financial assistance from the 21st Century Scholars program. I just had academic scholarships and a few grants from the lovely state of Indiana.

You're probably wondering why I don't have the 21st Century Scholar's financial assistance offered to low-income students in Indiana. Believe me, my family more than qualified for it, but I never believed that I could be one of the people who could pursue a higher education in college. I was fixed on working at a fast food chain and maybe if I worked hard enough I could become the manager someday. Therefore, I didn't sign up for the scholarship in the 8th grade.

I surprised myself when I fell in love with IPFW

through the college preparatory program Upward Bound. Upward Bound is a program that aims to serve high school students from low-income families and from families in which neither parent holds a bachelor's degree. Upon high school graduation, I thought this was supposed to feel like this was one of the best days of my life, but it wasn't. I was not satisfied with accomplishing high school like I thought I would be; maybe, that was because Upward Bound told me I was capable of so much more enough times that it actually stuck. Now, I wouldn't be satisfied unless I graduated from college. One of my biggest concerns about coming to college, though, was how I was actually going to pay for things. Yes, I had a nice award letter; but, that was only enough to cover tuition and my student housing. I still had to eat.

People ask me all the time why I moved out of my home if I only live 15 minutes from IPFW, especially since money was a concern. My senior year of high school, my single mother of three children (of whom I was the youngest) wanted to get back out on the dating scene. Unfortunately for us, my mother had horrible taste in men. Her new beau moved in with us about a month after I had met him for the first time. As the facade always ends, we later discovered he was an abusive alcoholic. "Lorenzo, it's not like he hits me; he just gets stupid when he drinks," my mom said. "Don't pay him any mind; it will only make him worse." This was a problem because I cannot stand by and let things happen. I cannot allow a man to speak to my mother the way that he did—in such a demeaning and belittling way. For those reasons, I was targeted by him. He called me a stupid little bitch and told me there was no reason to go to college because I'd never be anything. Honestly, all of that hurt; but, I also know that people project their own feelings. What hurt the most was the fact that my mom would just stand there and tell me that I was making it worse by trying to stand up for her. I then knew, in order to succeed in college and to remain somewhat sane, I needed to move out.

As I was saying before, one of my concerns was paying for things, especially food because I did not have a car to get back and forth to the grocery store. Luckily for me, college is the great equalizer where we are all tired, broke, and hungry. IPFW must have known this common similarity between college students because they would often hold workshops on numerous topics from: building your résumé, learning about graduate school, leadership training, studying abroad, etc.—all with free food. My slogan became, "I came for the food but stay for the information." As I did that, I learned so much. I learned about TRIO Student Support Services (SSS) which is like Upward Bound but for college students—there to help students succeed and get to graduation. TRIO SSS helped me in so many ways with maintaining my sanity in college and offering opportunities—even one that would take me across the North Atlantic Ocean to Salamanca, Spain and another experience to San Juan, Puerto Rico. My TRIO advisor knew I was interested in the field of health care and pointed me in the direction of a student organization known as Global Health Initiative—which focused on global health issues. In addition to learning about events from my amazing TRIO advisor, I would look on billboards or offices for posters in my scavenge for daily food. I came to receive my Leadership 102 certificate after attending a semester's worth of leadership workshops where I learned about self-growth and improvement. Later, I went to the Global Leadership Summit where I heard speakers such as T.D. Jakes, Melinda Gates, John C. Maxwell, Dr. Travis Bradberry, and many more.

On Wednesdays, the Anthropology Club met and offered a number of interesting topics by guest speakers and one was especially interesting. At one of the anthropology meetings, one of the professors came to speak on the research she had been doing. At the time, I didn't know who she was, but later I came to find out that the talk she gave at the Anthropology Club was a rehearsal for her TEDx Talk in Naperville, Illinois. Hispanos Unidos (Hispanics United) was another club I explored on campus—again because they had free food. Being involved in Hispanos Unidos brought me to the Office of Diversity and Multicultural Affairs (ODMA). ODMA is where I would come to meet some of my closest friends, be given the opportunity to attend health conferences, and become exposed to the Hispanic Leadership Coalition of Northeast Indiana (HLCNI)—that later awarded me scholarships totaling $2,000. I have come to realize that there are endless opportunities available at IPFW, and I discovered them all because I needed to find free food on campus. Opportunities are available; you just have to be open to recognizing them. I now have an on-campus job so the need to scavenge for food isn't as vital. But in that search for food, I found so many more things than I had ever thought I would.

Never forget, you're not who the critics say you are; you're so much more than that. You can do anything in this world because no one knows you, but you. The reason every low-income or minority student should go to college is because there are so many opportunities out there that we may not even realize exist. We are already used to being tired, broke, and hungry so why not do it for four more years pursuing a higher education and soaking up all of the opportunities along the way? Then, you'll no longer be tired, broke, and hungry ever again.

Stay strong, Mom, I'll always love you, no matter what.

NOT OKAY
BY MEGAN PEARSALL

My whole life I knew I was not as okay as I should be. I really realized it my first year of college. I thought when I graduated from high school my worrying and overthinking would be at ease. Everyone worries and overthinks from time-to-time, but I do it almost every single day. Even when life is going beautifully and I have nothing I should worry about, I still manage to find something.

I have always been this person; but, my first year of college it got worse. I would find myself having random panic attacks—no reason for them—just random. Some days, I would find myself just having trouble breathing; but, I would just take deep breaths and be okay. Other days were much scarier because I would end up collapsing to the floor because I could not get any air. I felt hot, my stomach in knots, my mind dizzy, lightheaded, and seeing spots. No matter how hard I tried, I never had the words to explain what anxiety and depression feels like. It isn't just sadness for a day. There are different forms of it. Things were even harder when others felt like what I was feeling and how I acted was all for attention. At least, that's how I felt everyone else viewed it.

My second semester, I slowly started to figure things out. I got the help I needed just by talking to different members of TRIO, my friends, family, and boyfriend. They all helped me get through my daily battles with anxiety. It is hard sometimes for them, I know, but just having the support made a big difference. My hope for writing this is to encourage all of the people who deal with the same feelings I do, to get help or just talk to someone about everything. My other hope—for those reading who don't deal with these thoughts and feelings but know of someone who does—is to encourage you to be a listener. Just by listening and telling someone things will get better and helping them along the way, you might even be saving a life. I know now, that everything will be okay because even when it doesn't feel like it, I take a deep breath and reach out for help.

CAUTION: ROADBLOCK AHEAD
BY MIRANDA HALL

I came from a family of young parents. My grandparents and parents both had children at a young age. This caused my family to go straight into working to provide for their families; and, that resulted in no one attending college. Except me. I am the first one to step foot into a college and try to get my degree.

We had some money, but never a lot. I always remember my parents living paycheck to paycheck to pay the bills. They always made sure we had what we needed, but I knew we struggled. When the trailer industry went, so did my dad's job. Later on, my dad was able to get another job and things seemed to look up; but, then went my mother's job.

I was always told if you wanted something you have to work for it. It wasn't just going to fall into your lap. And so I did. Since the age of 14, I have had my own job. A job that you have to pay taxes on—not just yard work or babysitting here and there. I did those things too, but I knew I needed something else. I knew my parents were not always going to be able to pay for everything, so I did what I could. My first job was cleaning offices at a nursing home where I worked with my mom. This was her second or third job at the time, trying to make ends meet. We were only allowed to work 13 hours a week between the both of us, earning $7.25 each. You can imagine how long it would take to save up for much. But I kept working. I worked and worked until I finally saved up for my very own laptop. It was a bulky, old, black Dell that now would be obsolete. But to me, it was an accomplishment. The feeling of purchasing your own things with money you have earned is greatly satisfying.

The other struggle I have faced is not having my driver's license. You are probably thinking...really? No license? Yes, I am that one person who has yet to get my license. A lot of it has to do with money; but, the other bit is due to anxiety that being in vehicles gives me. It's the one thing I have struggled with since turning 16 until now at the age of 22. It's something that I'm very hopeful about in the near future, but still always seems too far out of sight.

Never once have my parents told me I was a burden. But the feeling of being a burden does come when you know you don't always have the money to do things, yet you do them anyways. When you can buy your own things, the burden now falls away from your family. When I buy my own things, I feel like I am not taking away from my parents or my little brother. Even though, I know my parents just want the best for me, and would do anything for me, there is still that feeling of burden. Since my first job, I have gone from having one job to three at a time. But, the way I get through it is knowing I can take care of myself and make the burden a little less for my family.

When I came to college, there money was again. The big blinking caution sign in front of me blocking my view.

Money. How will I pay for college? How is this going to affect my family? Is it possible? Money, again, was the main issue. In addition, I was going to school to be a teacher, which means I hear at least once a week "does not make much money." Which I know, obviously, but this time I'm determined not to let money ruin that for me. My love for teaching children has overpowered the desire to make money. So when I started college, I said I would do anything to accomplish my dreams. Now, as a junior in college I am working hard in school and working three jobs right now. But while I'm doing that, I'm also keeping in mind at the end, it'll all be worth it. As for my parents, they have gotten jobs at a great company and have stable positions that help a little more with bills than before. This reminds me to keep pressing forward because things do get better, even when they don't seem like they ever will. It's like driving down a small dirt road with the hope that it will bring you back to the interstate. Finally, in the distance you see it and know you are going in the right direction.

Money has always been the headlights that blind me when I think about my future. But, seeing how my parents persevere shows me that things sometimes just take a little while. With the help of my parents and some amazing people in my life, I know that even though money will always be in my rearview mirror reminding me that it is there, I can still keep driving and know it's not the only thing I have in my path.

THE STORY OF A SMILE
BY RILEY ERCK

I have always adored teeth. It's a passion that many find weird, but improving one little smile can change an entire life. As a child, my teeth were brittle (thanks genetics); plus, I also enjoyed sugar more than I should have. I practically lived at the dentist's and didn't want it any other way. I never quite understood why people think of the dental office as a horrifying place that must be avoided at all costs. My childhood dentist and his staff were always friendly and welcoming. They never failed to remember who I was and the events that were happening in my life. They made me feel like a part of the family. Getting a toy as a 'prize' after each visit also didn't hurt.

In middle school, I was bullied due to my appearance; having a big gap between my two front teeth and a snaggle tooth creeping in on top of an already existing cuspid didn't help either. Getting braces in eighth grade dramatically boosted my confidence and added to my positive experiences with members of the dental community. Each individual in the office cared for their patient's well-being. I was also commended on how well I was taking care of my teeth and braces. Most people cannot wait to get their braces removed; I, however, was sad to see them go—knowing they would be missed. Having a newly renovated smile was a great change to my self-esteem. I no longer feared what others thought; I now saw myself as worthy and beautiful. Directly experiencing how changing a smile's appearance can boost one's confidence and positively affect an individual's outlook on life deepened my love for dentistry even more.

Ever since a young age, I knew I enjoyed the dental environment but was unsure if I had what it took to become a member myself. My memory is awful; would I be able to remember details about my patients to make them feel as comfortable as my dentist had for me? Would I be able to handle temporarily causing pain so that in the long haul my patient could feel better? Would I be able to go home every day knowing that some hate my profession and dread coming to see me? It was not until I gained more knowledge and hands-on training that I realized being a part of the dental field truly was my calling.

My junior year of high school, I attended Anthis Career Center, a technical school which provided a half-day dental class. The teacher of the class has since become a very near and dear person in my life. I will forever credit her with my exploration into my love for the dental field. Her immense amount of passion, both for dental career—as well as— her students, has inspired and motivated me to reach for the stars. She has continually mentored me through the obstacles associated with college and helped me prepare for a School of Dentistry. Without her, I am sure my life would be missing not only a positive role model, but also a kind soul who truly cares. In her dental class, we explored different fields of density, medical terminology, dental instruments, anatomy, and so much more. We did this all while practicing hands-on dental procedures such as setting up a dental unit, interacting with patients, disinfecting and sterilization, taking and filling impressions, and placing amalgam (metal) and composite (tooth colored) fillings.

Acquiring all of this dental knowledge allowed me to participate in the 2014 HOSA Future Health Professional's competition. This competition started at the state level. All juniors and seniors who attended a medical class at a technical school were invited to compete. I traveled to Indianapolis, Indiana along with many other eager and nervous students, excited to prove our knowledge while meeting others just like us from different areas. We were tested in comprehensive knowledge of our medical field, as well as, the skills acquired for said fields. This was an amazing experience to just be a part of, but by employing the skills I had learned, I placed second in the state of Indiana for dental skills. This was a tremendous accomplishment for me.

Placing in the top ten allowed me to continue on to nationals at HOSA's 37th Annual National Leadership Conference in Orlando, Florida. The top students from each state in each category would be tested in hopes of placement in the top ten of the entire United States. I wanted more than anything to be able to take place in this competition and prove to myself and others that dentistry is for me; however, trips can be expensive especially for a first-generation college student whose mom doesn't work. After confiding the unlikelihood of me being able to attend Nationals, my teacher immediately began to help me find a way to finance this trip of a lifetime.

Attending HOSA Nationals was one of the most reassuring experiences I have had. I was able to network in a professional setting with others from all around the country, as well as, participate in something I loved. Although I did not place in the top ten, I was able to fuel my passion and start on the journey towards a lifetime of dental success. I had, in turn, proved that my memory would not be an obstacle in the way of my dream career. Someday, I will be able to help patients by putting aside temporary discomfort in order to provide a healthier future. I will not take offense of other's dread caused by past bad experiences, but rather change those experiences for the better.

Now, I'm a junior in my second year of college, studying biology pre-dentistry with a concentration in microbiology and immunology and a minor in psychology. I still rely heavily on the teacher who helped me discover more about my passion. She continues to provide me with the motivation and confidence to power through the hard times and is a trusted confidant. Since attending Anthis, I have not only remained in contact with her, but I have also continually returned to her class. The past three years, I have been assisting students with dental skills in her lab. I enjoy the time I get to spend alongside her, helping the students nurture their passion as she has mine.

Thanks to her, I have found my forever career and my deep love for dentistry. She has not only helped me develop skills, but has also encouraged and enabled me to network with members of the dental field. She incites my drive to push through the struggles of college. My goal is to become one of the best general dentists, possibly specializing in orthodontics and forensic dentistry. I hope to change the stereotype surrounding dentistry and show the joy dentistry can bring patients. Maybe one day, I will teach dentistry at the university level giving back to the community just as my mentor does.

Since a young age, I have been someone who smiles bright. Because of a wonderful role-model, I am assured that I can brighten the smiles of others, too. I am blessed enough to have been pushed to follow my passion. She will forever be in my heart as a wonderful mentor, role model, and dear friend.

THE LIST OF UNCERTAINTY
BY TAYAH LUCKADOO

1. I feel like I don't belong here.

2. Not smart enough to achieve anything.

3. Not sure if I'm following my passion.

4. Don't even know what my passion is.

5. Afraid I'm making a mistake with my major.

6. But, don't have enough time to change it.

7. Because I only have four years till my scholarship expires.

8. Wasn't sure if I wanted to come to college in the first place.

9. However, I don't want to throw this opportunity away.

10. Parents expect me to break the dysfunctional cycle.

11. But, I'm not sure how to do that on my own.

12. Mom tried to finish college, couldn't.

13. Dad never went and worked at a factory all his life.

14. I've doubted myself since I can remember.

15. And, I have never dipped my toes beyond the surface.

16. Pushing myself to break the norm.

17. Teaching myself to be more assertive and confident.

18. I'll be on my own soon, getting ready to leave the nest.

19. Can't be weak in this world.

20. But, I'm not perfect and I'm still learning.

21. But, I discovered something.

22. I'm stronger than I think.

23. I do everything on my own and I'm not completely failing.

24. I make every final choice.

25. I have achieved a 3.50/4.00, highest GPA I've ever had.

26. I've made the Dean's List with little hope.

27. I've made the Honors List with little sleep.

28. I have excelled to my surprise, working one or more jobs.

29. Despite my family issues, I am kind to everyone (who is kind to me).

30. I refuse to let my anger change me.

31. Because, I know I'm the only one I can control.

32. And, how my life turns out is through no one's fault but my own.

33. So, I'm going to do it on my own.

34. Why?

35. Because I can.

NOW WHAT?
BY TIFFANY LACKEY

I graduated with my bachelor's degree in general studies, along with minors in psychology, sociology, and women's studies, on December 15, 2015. Throughout the five and a half years that it took me to graduate, I had my share of setbacks: I failed half my classes my freshman year; I changed my major and department not once, not twice, but three times; and my depression wreaked havoc on my academic and personal life. But through it all, and with the help of my friends, family, and TRIO Student Support Services, I persevered.

Now what? I've graduated, shouldn't I have had a plan? Shouldn't I already be set on a path towards the career I want? Shouldn't I have had *some* semblance of an idea of what I wanted to do? Should, should, should; but I didn't. I was faced with a choice: keep going to school or attempt to get an adult job and live an actual adult life. I chose the former, and decided to apply to grad school. But, I didn't really know what I wanted to do. I mean, I had the idea that I wanted to help people, but I wasn't sure in what capacity. So, I decided to check out all of my options. Spoiler alert: there were a LOT. Turns out if you've got a bachelor's degree you can apply to get any master's degree you want! That was both a blessing and a curse. I had all the doors open to me, but no clue where to start. So, I started at the grad office that was literally the closest to me at the time and got as much info about that program as I could. Then, I just went to the next department, and the next, and the next, and... you get the picture.

Once I had all the info on all the grad programs at IPFW, I started sorting through them. Science and biology were out because I never excelled at those; engineering was out because I should not be trusted to build a bridge or anything that could electrocute me; and math was out before I even picked up the info. One program that stuck out to me was the Education and Public Policy department, but I was hesitant to apply because I thought I had to have a teaching background to get in (which was not the case). After perusing the website and the material the office assistant gave me, I knew this was the place for me. I even had the option to specialize in either school counseling or marriage and family counseling.

I knew I wanted to help people like me. Growing up, I didn't have strong academic support. My mental illness (depression) was put on the back burner because we didn't know how to deal with it; and no one in my family identified as queer, so I was alone on that one too. I knew I wanted to be there for people who felt left behind in some way. I decided I wanted to be a high school counselor but had no idea how to go about applying for grad school.

Did you know that many graduate programs require the Graduate Record Examination (GRE) if your GPA isn't at a certain level? Because I didn't, until I wanted to apply to grad school. My GPA didn't hit the minimum requirements to get into the program without taking the GRE, so I had to take it. The GRE is basically the SAT amped to the max. You have to schedule a time to take it, which needs to be at least three weeks before the scores are due so they can be submitted on time. The exam is split into three sections, costs about $200 to take, and I did not do well.

Even though I didn't do stellar on the GRE, I submitted the scores with my application—along with a laundry list of other forms and paperwork. Included were the GRE scores, official transcripts from my current university, and an application fee. Just *applying* to grad school cost $263, and that doesn't even guarantee you a spot in the program. I should know; I was rejected.

No explanation, just a letter basically saying "Thanks, but no thanks." I had built up this entire plan on what I was going to do once I got in: I was going to kick butt in the classes, get a rad internship at a school that wanted to hire me as soon as I graduated, and start making an impact in students' lives. That idea wasn't just ripped from my grasp; it was beaten within an inch of its life right before my eyes. For a few weeks, I was done with anything that had to do with grad school, or school in general—which was fun considering I was working at a university. One of the coordinators in TRIO kept asking me if I had gotten in touch with anyone in the department to see why I had been rejected, and I kept putting it off because—oh boy, was I bitter.

I finally bit the bullet and sent one of the heads of the department and the administrative assistant an email asking why I wasn't accepted. They told me that since my GPA didn't meet the minimum requirements (it was 0.08 points away from the minimum), they didn't even **look** at my application. Again, bitter. But the head of the department that I emailed sent me something back that I did not expect. She told me that one of the students who had been accepted into the school counseling program had deferred her enrollment, and there was one spot still open. I was curious what this meant for me, because I had been rejected on the basis of my GPA and was sure that having an open spot wasn't going to change anything. After further correspondence, I was informed that I could be admitted into the program as a conditional student—on a trial-basis. I would complete at least 9 credit hours (3 classes), maintain at least a 3.0 GPA, and have to pay for the classes out-of-pocket.

I was all for it until that last part. I'm a recent college graduate who works part time at a university, making less than it would cost to pay for graduate tuition for the entire year. There was absolutely no way this was happening, and I could feel it slipping away again. I had gotten my hopes up too many times and this was it, the straw that would break the camel's back. I talked to the financial aid department and there was no aid that a conditional student could receive. I couldn't afford it on my own as it was, and I couldn't get enough saved up in time even if I got a second and a third job.

I am incredibly lucky to have the family that I do because they offered to foot the bill for my first two semesters. My grandma took out a personal loan to do repairs on her house and gave me enough to pay for my summer courses and books, and my mom withdrew from her retirement fund to pay for my fall courses. Without these two helping me, there is no way I would have been able to even THINK about grad school.

Attending classes in a program that you're not technically in is daunting. I felt like I had to get the best grades, that I was being scrutinized more than my classmates, and that I had something to prove. After the summer and fall semesters were over, I had a meeting with my professors to determine if I would go on to be fully admitted into the program. They sat in a semi-circle around me and asked me a ton of questions. I went into the meeting thinking that they would let me know their decision in an email a week later—but nope—they deliberated in front of me, and let me know their decision right then and there. I was sure I would get a "Thanks for trying, but you're not really counselor material," but that didn't happen. Instead, I heard, "I think we're all agreed that we would like to welcome you into the school counseling program."

Currently, I am pursuing my Masters of Science degree in Education with a concentration in school counseling at IPFW—earning straight As. Most of the time, it's stressful and I want to scream into a pillow when I think about writing ANOTHER twenty page paper; but overall, it's worth it. It's worth it because soon I will be able to help students who feel like they have no help.

BEFORE IT'S TOO LATE
BY YIN THET

My first semester of college was terrible. I did not manage my time well. I never went to class. I never did my homework. I never studied. I never asked questions. But most importantly, I never asked for help.

Growing up as the oldest child in my family, and only having my dad until I was 13, I had to help everyone in my family with everything. My mom was not in a good place after my dad died. She had trouble taking care of herself. So around that time, I felt it was my responsibility to take care of my family. I helped schedule appointments, take my mom places and take my siblings to school activities, cook, clean, and go grocery shopping. I never said, "No, this is too much for me to do." I just said yes and did whatever I could to make things easier for my mom—who was now a single mother raising three children. I never asked for help because it made me feel weak. I did not want others to see me stress out or cry. I just put a smile on my face and acted like I was doing great and I could handle everything.

After seeing my first semester grades, I could tell I wasn't doing great. I had 3 Cs, a D, and an F. It lowered my GPA a great deal. This was when I broke down. Some people might not think this was a big deal and would have brushed it off. Failure to me is when I know my mom would be disappointed with these grades. I also always had As and Bs in high school, so this was a big drop.

I was helping my family, but not myself. The grades made me realize that I needed to help myself first; but when I said that to myself, I felt… selfish. I was raised to put my family before myself. My parents emigrated from Burma and they gave up everything so we could have a better education and future. Knowing their sacrifice and what they did to make our lives easier, I just felt like I had to give back and help my mom as much as I could. My grades made me realize that I shouldn't have to do this all the time. I cannot just forget about myself otherwise their sacrifice would have been for nothing. I needed to find the middle ground.

I was the first in my family to go to preschool, elementary school, middle school, high school, and—finally—the first in my family to go to college. Being first meant I was to set an example for my siblings. I realized I couldn't show them that failure is good; but, also I did not want them to think it was bad. To me, failure meant I had to fix what I had been doing wrong. It meant a second chance. It meant I needed to ask for help.

I started going to my advisors, talking to my teachers when I was struggling, asking my classmates for help and finally asking my mom for help. These little things made such a big difference in my second semester. All these things I did not do before, helped me pass all my classes the next semester. I had all As and one B. It helped me raise my GPA and made my mom proud. I realized, in that moment, helping myself was also helping my mom and my family. I realized it meant asking for help was not a sign of weakness, but something I had to ask for.

Now, I am a sophomore in the elementary education program with an additional certificate to Teach English as a New Language (TENL). My mom and I have split the responsibilities, so it is easier for me to go to school and get good grades. Whenever I feel like I will not meet deadlines or I am too stressed, I talk to my teachers and they help me by giving extensions or showing me how to make it easier on myself. I de-stress by hanging out with my friends and making time for me. I make sure to ask for help before it is too late.

FIRST
BY ANITA VANNATTA

This is a story of firsts. Although we have many firsts in our life, this particular story is about being the first in my family to earn a bachelor's degree. It all began with that first dinner I could not eat: family I had lived near my whole life surrounded the table at my favorite Chinese restaurant. Friends and relatives were wishing me the very best as they were saying good-bye. How could I do this? What was I thinking? Going over 2,000 miles away from home to a place I had never been, to live with people I had never met! Was I crazy? Nothing, not even my favorite restaurant could bring me to eat. My stomach was in knots. Mom seemed to understand as she patiently accepted the fact that there was food left on my plate. In just a few days, I would pack up my belongings and ship them ahead of myself to a university in Indiana. All those brave statements of: "I can't wait to get out of here" seemed to echo and disappear into a sea of doubt. Nevertheless, I was committed as an incoming freshman, the financial aid package accepted, and plane tickets in hand. Like it or not, this was going to happen.

The next big first was a five and a half hour plane flight from Idaho to Indiana. As I boarded the plane, my focus was on finding a seat without making eye contact while pretending I had done this a million times before. In my seat, I alienated and protected myself with my Walkman, headphones, and reading material. Sitting by the window offered an ideal place to watch the mountains disappear into the flat lands of the Midwest. I had never been on a plane before and wondered what it would be like to fly for so many hours and navigate singlehandedly the massive airport in Chicago. My stomach was a mess; I did not want to leave my parents. As I held back the tears and tried not to cry, the pilot began speaking and the flight attendants began to show us emergency procedures. My next thought was please do not crash!

Growing up, my grandpa repeatedly told me I would go to Huntington University even though it is so far away. Maybe he was to blame for this knot in my stomach! Maybe I should stay in Idaho and follow my classmates to the local college. Yet, enduring another four years of the same people and maintaining the status quo really did not sound very attractive to me. I wondered why I felt the strong pull to be different. Maybe it was the support of my parents and other family members telling me that I could do anything. Mom kept telling me to get that degree, that magical piece of paper that would bring a better life for me and my family, no matter what! I had internalized my experiences growing up to live a different life. I wanted to build a future where I didn't have to tell my kids "no you cannot have that because I don't have the money" every time they expressed a desire to take dance lessons or go to a camp or take a class. I wanted to have freedom, options, and feel successful. I did not want to work in a factory forever, wondering if I would be next to be downsized like my dad did for so many years. The plane engine revved and the doors locked shut. The flight attendants prepared for takeoff. When I looked real close, I could see at the window mom and dad watching and waving. When will I see them again? How alone I felt on that plane. The plane began moving, then faster and faster. My head pushed back against the seat as the nose rose away from the ground. No turning back now. We went higher and higher until we eventually leveled out and my ears began to pop.

That first night was quite memorable. Only certain upper classmen and athletes were on campus. I was alone in a room that was half the size of my room back home. I approached everything as a quiet, cautious, suspicious and guarded freshman, taking in all the new sights. Some upperclassmen were friendly and offered to sit with me at dinner and show me around campus. I was waiting for the other freshmen to come for their big move in day. For now, I was on my own in a humid, flat, and mostly deserted campus. Finally, I made my first long distance phone call home to ease my nerves with the encouraging voices of my parents saying, "Don't quit!"

First meetings: Move in day brought a flurry of people with family and so many items for their rooms. I only had a few boxes that had come via UPS. All of which had been quickly unpacked and placed in the small dresser, desk, and closet. Some photos of family and loved ones lined the shelf. The new students were friendly, happy, and excited. I wondered if they would like me and if I would fit in. A sadness still lingered on what I left behind. The knots in my stomach were there; but, they began to disappear as I made friends and experienced my first session of classes, my first dinner with other students, and my first job on campus. Things were beginning to fall into a pattern and instead of everything being a first; it became routine.

Being first can be the best thing to happen to you. It

can be the scariest thing that can happen to you; but do not let that stop you. College is full of firsts, some wonderful, some hurtful, some joyful and some sorrowful, but all worth it! Why not face the challenge? Be bold, set your course and experience many firsts until you make a difference. Looking back, it was the best time of my life and the best decision I ever made. I have only met a tiny handful of people who were brave enough to do the same thing I did. You never know what taking that first step could lead to. Here is a list of other firsts that resulted from me being first in my family to go to college. As you can see, many of them are not what you would expect to read in college marketing material!

- First time in a chicken coop, on a dairy farm in Pennsylvania during Thanksgiving break.
- First time to hear kettledrums, see the Southern Cross and snorkel in the Caribbean Ocean on a mission trip.
- First time to see the Atlantic Ocean and run on Myrtle Beach in North Carolina during spring break training for track and field.
- First time in Kentucky, Pennsylvania, Texas, Florida, Ohio, Illinois, North Carolina, and the Virgin Islands.
- First time to earn a 3.4 GPA, pull an all-nighter, study psychology, and write a research paper.
- Fist time to hear classical music performed live on stage by a full orchestra.
- First time to visit a cathedral, an art museum, and Washington D.C.
- First time elected class vice president and homecoming representative.
- First time to hold a school athletic record, run in the snow and start a relay team.
- First time with friends 24/7 just outside my

door!
- First time to take a photograph for the cover of the yearbook and first time to perform on stage.
- Then, in May, I walked across the stage with my first bachelor's degree as my friends and family cheered me on!

Do not be afraid to make your own story of firsts.

THE GOOD FIGHT
BY KAREN LENFESTEY

Neither of my parents graduated from high school, yet they always taught me to respect my teachers. My father worked in the oil fields which was a tough, dirty job that supported my two brothers, my sister and me. At one point, my dad was offered a job with benefits in the office of the oil company, but he was afraid his lack of education would show, so he turned it down.

My mother worked hard at home, cooking, sweeping and mopping the kitchen daily. My brothers' friends hung out at our house so much they called her "Mom Snyder" and my mom never knew how many kids were there until she cooked breakfast in the morning.

Since he travelled a lot for work, my dad encouraged my sister and me to look out for each other. He told us kids, "I don't ever want to see you start a fight, but I don't ever want to see you run from one, either." When my sister was old enough for first grade, he sent me along even though I was a year younger. Fortunately, I managed to keep up with the work. When we graduated high school,

I asked if I could go to college, but my father said only if my sister and I went to the same school. My sister wanted to be a nurse and I wanted to be a teacher and so he said neither of us could go. I begged him to let me go, but he wouldn't budge. I asked my mother, but she always backed my father. At this point, my sister gave up on the idea, but this was a fight I wasn't going to run from. Determined to make my dreams come true, I went to our neighbor and asked if I could borrow some money for tuition. I don't know why, but he said yes. I enrolled in college and was so excited to start my studies. When my dad found out about the loan, he was mad but he paid the neighbor back. He also decided to let me stay in school.

I loved learning and playing tennis in college. My junior year I fell in love with a boy on the football team. We started dating and ended up getting married. When I became pregnant, we both quit school to get jobs. I gave birth to a baby girl, followed later by two boys. As I worked doing other people's laundry, I never forgot about my goal of becoming a teacher. Ten years after I left school, my husband and I went to talk to the college advisor about our credits. Since I was closer to graduating than he was, we decided that I would finish my degree. Soon I graduated and was doing what I loved, teaching elementary children how to read and count. (My husband never did finish his degree.)

I was so proud a few years later when my daughter graduated early from high school just so she could enroll in the local college. Then, her daughter grew up *knowing* that college was in her future. Eventually all three of us went on to earn master's degrees—mine in education, my daughter's in anthropology and my granddaughter's in counseling. Because I fought to be the first in my family to go to college, it has had a ripple effect on future generations. Who knows? Maybe my great-granddaughter will be the first in the family to earn a doctorate!

This is the story of my Grandma Ruth, who loved children the way all teachers and grandmothers should. I always enjoyed hearing the story of how she defied her father and borrowed $50 from the neighbor so she could go to college. I didn't find out about her long detour before graduation described here until I was an adult. All I knew growing up was that she was a college graduate. Because of her, I never doubted that I could make it in college, too.

AN OPPORTUNITY TO CHANGE A LIFE
BY SHUBITHA KEVER

My first weeks of college were much different than I expected. I had heard stories and watched movies that showed how fun college life was going to be. You got to engage with esteemed professors, learn really interesting things, meet friends you would have for a lifetime, and experience freedom like you never knew before. My college experience was much different.

I did well in high school academically. I won awards and liked learning on a much deeper level than most high school students. I read philosophy books for fun, and I loved working on logic puzzles and solving problems.

I never questioned if I would go to college; but to be honest, I never knew how much I didn't know about going to college until the summer after my high school graduation. I had applied to colleges when my friends told me they were applying earlier that fall. Their parents helped them and they helped me. I got accepted by every college I applied to; but in reality, that was only two. I

79

chose those two colleges because my friends were applying to those colleges and I didn't know much about any others.

My first big blow came when the colleges asked for financial documents and payments. I got the award letters from each of the colleges saying how much aid I would get from each. And even though I was going to get a small amount of aid because I had good grades, it was nowhere near the total cost of attendance. I was in the middle gap. My parents made too much money for me to qualify for any grants or income-based scholarships but not enough to pay for my college expenses.

The next thing I got in the mail from the university was a letter asking: *How do you plan on paying for college?* I didn't want to ask my parents about that because I already knew there was no *plan* to pay for college. My parents had not ever been in a situation to make a plan for that. It was, then, that I realized my friends and I were much more different than I had always thought. As they selected their colleges, I watched as our lives began to divide. Me on one side of the giant crack in the Earth and them on the other. I listened as they talked about their parents making arrangements for them to live on campuses across the state, set-up food plans, and open bank accounts for *other* expenses.

So, when July finally came around and I couldn't make any of the initial payments for housing or tuition that colleges required, I was out. My *place* at the university was no longer being *held*. I helped my friends pack up and go away to start their exciting college journeys, and I was left behind.

Even with the disappointment of all that was happening in my life, I tried to stay positive. It was about that time too, that my parents thought I should get a job. That's what they had done at 18 years old; so, that's what they thought I should do too. My mom got me a job in the factory she had worked at for almost 20 years already. She was able to get me a secretarial job in the factory: filing papers, answering phones, and typing reports. And although I appreciated what she had done, I hated working there. Most of the people who worked there did so because they had to, not because they wanted to. Many had few other options or choices because they had no education, connections, or specialized skills. And, watching the physicality of the tasks take a toll on their bodies was hard. It was then that I decided this factory might be my beginning, but it wasn't going to be my end.

It was around that time that I heard about a local university that was within driving distance: IPFW. And so, I decided to check it out. Everything I had heard up until then was that only people who couldn't get into other colleges went there. I assumed it was for remedial students. I had no idea how wrong I was.

I went to the campus in late summer to see if I could still start that fall. When I came to campus, there were barely any people there. I remember walking the empty halls alone and wondering if I would ever find the places I needed to go or if I would ever meet any friends. I had to apply for student loans because that was the only option I had available to me. And on top of that, I ended up with a horrible schedule because early classes were the only ones still available this close to the semester beginning. But, through it all, people at the university helped me get ready to start in just a few short weeks. And while many looked over their counters at me with furrowed brows for not having the right paperwork and for submitting every application paper late, I pressed on. While they viewed me as a task to complete; I viewed this as a chance to change my life...and possibly, that of my family too.

My first weeks on campus were just as challenging. The campus was largely commuter, so like a lot of other students, I would drive to classes and leave right after. I had no time to meet anyone. I had a schedule where I would work all day in the factory three days out of the week and I would go to school the other two. But with the horrible schedule I got at the last minute, I had to also take an accelerated, French, night class two nights a week which just happened to be on the days I worked at the factory. So, I ended up having to drive to campus 4 days a week. The factory was the opposite direction from the campus too, so I spent almost 2 hours in my car every day.

That schedule took a toll on me. And, finding time to study wasn't always easy. It didn't help that we didn't have a computer at home for a long time either. My parents saw a computer and internet as luxuries that were like games—unnecessary. But, my instructors would insist we use the computer to turn in homework, email, and even type our papers. So, I spent hours that first semester in computer labs on campus, just trying to do my homework. And add to all that, I still hadn't made one friend.

That first semester didn't get any easier. I didn't make any friends, my grades weren't as good as they could have been, and I drifted farther and farther away from my high school friends because I couldn't relate to their experiences anymore. When they would come home for breaks, I would be working. And when they would talk about their experiences—all the parties and friends they had made, I couldn't relate because my experience was so different.

Nevertheless, I refused to give up. I enrolled in classes the next semester earlier, tried to fix my schedule as best I could, and begged my parents to get a working computer. I started the semester knowing I needed to pick a major, make some friends, and find a way to get those lost connections with people back—because being a loner was never really my thing. And by the next fall, I had made some friends; joined a campus group; and had a few professors who showed genuine interest in helping me navigate the processes of college that I had been treading on my own for the last year.

What I learned from all this is that things are likely not going to turn out how you imagined them. But just because you may not end up where you thought you would be doesn't mean you didn't end up where you were supposed to be. The college I attended ended up being a really wonderful place to be—and I am so glad there was an option for me so close by. It gave me a world of opportunities I wasn't expecting and helped me make connections with people I never thought I would. But, none of that came quickly or easily. If I had given up—like I thought so much about that first semester—I wouldn't be where I am today or who I am today.

Speaking of today, I've come full circle. I now work on that very campus helping students who have similar struggles to my own. I try to help answer their questions, help students think of creative solutions to their problems, let students know much brighter times are ahead, and that others have gone before them and are ready and willing to help them now. And above all else, I make sure those students know I never see them as a task to be completed, but always as *an opportunity to change a life*.

ABOUT THE AUTHORS

This collection of stories was written by TRIO students and staff at Indiana University-Purdue University in Fort Wayne, Indiana (IPFW). Some of the students are freshmen, some are recent graduates or somewhere in-between, but all are part of TRIO Student Support Services—a federally-funded program that offers support to students who are the first in their families to pursue a college degree.